EDUCATION IN
THE GRAPHIC ARTS

A symposium held in the Wiggin Gallery,

Boston Public Library, on May 5, 1967

Education in the Graphic Arts

The speakers and their subjects:

RAY NASH
The Undergraduate and the Graphic Arts

FRITZ EICHENBERG
The Education of a Graphic Artist

FREDERICK WALKEY
Graphic Arts Education: A Museum Program

BOSTON   1969

The symposium *Education in the Graphic Arts* and the publication of this book have been made possible through the support and encouragement of the Albert H. and Jessie D. Wiggin Foundation.

FOREWORD

THE world of activity in the graphic arts should be construed to include not only the practitioner but also the student, collector, dealer and scholar. The artist, the calligrapher, the type designer share interests with the art historian, the librarian, the teacher. The bookseller and printseller, the publisher, the book designer, the printer, the papermaker and many others in fields which include advertising and museum work all share certain interests in the graphic arts.

Many of these different people learn their skills and pursue their interests by apprenticeship rather than formal training. The evolution of the alphabet, the development of printing and printmaking processes, and our great humanistic tradition in the design and making of books, receive little recognition in the teaching of universities or in the honors they bestow.

With this in mind, we at the Boston Public Library sought out three men who are outstanding in their efforts to promote teaching in the graphic arts. Ray Nash's discovery of the directness of experience that occurs in a graphic arts workshop led him to establish a workshop at Dartmouth College when he began teaching there. In thirty years at Dartmouth he has had extraordinary influence. His students have become teachers, collectors, designers, publishers, printers and curators. Others not professionally engaged in printing and the graphic arts have retained, through him, an interest in book design, book production and graphic processes. He is a designer and printer as well as teacher, and as a scholar he has produced books and articles which are important contributions to knowledge in his field.

3

Most artists express themselves more easily in visual images than in words, but Fritz Eichenberg is articulate not only as a graphic artist but as a speaker, writer and editor. The Pratt Institute's Center for Contemporary Printmaking owes its beginnings to his efforts, and much of its current usefulness and vitality must be credited to his influence as well. Since 1966 he has been head of the Art Department of the University of Rhode Island. He and Professor Nash are among the very few teachers in America whose work gives young people an opportunity to enter the world of the graphic arts. Both men are humanists, and as teachers they must be counted pioneers.

As director of the DeCordova and Dana Museum, Frederick Walkey reaches out to an audience of all ages, offering them the chance to see original works of art and to try their own capacities as draughtsmen, painters, sculptors, printmakers. Few museums have a more ambitious teaching program. Among the teachers, artists predominate; a wealth of studio classes gives an introduction to different techniques and opportunities to practise them. Serving a suburban audience, the DeCordova is in the vanguard of American institutions which are opening the way to the fruitful use of our growing leisure.

We are grateful to Professor Nash, Professor Eichenberg, and Mr. Walkey for an extremely interesting symposium and for providing us with texts which the Library is pleased to publish.

PHILIP J. MCNIFF
Director, Boston Public Library

RAY NASH

The Undergraduate
and the Graphic Arts

FIRST of all, what do we mean by the liberal arts? the graphic arts?

Liberal arts presents no serious problem of definition. The term was already in use in fourteenth-century England to denote areas of scholarship worthy of a free man's attention, as distinct from servile and mechanic arts. In current educational talk it sets off the studies intended to broaden and refine intellectual powers from those that train the student for a particular profession or vocation. The liberal arts college undergraduate more often than not expects to go on to graduate school or to enter on-the-job training—unless the military snatches him first.

Graphic arts does not settle into place quite so comfortably. Too frequently—clipped to "graphics," a word once applied to the varieties of drawing and especially engineering draftsmanship—it tries to say prints or printmaking. It does not succeed in displacing these useful, unambiguous words, well worth defending against the encroachment of the sort of photo-mechanical painting reproductions that like to call themselves art prints. Properly, the graphic arts can be defined as those concerned with the making or manifolding of visual symbols based on writing or drawing. Calligraphy and drawing are at the center of the field of graphic art; perhaps Chinese painting would rank foremost in satisfying the definition fully. On the other hand photography, in spite of the misleading suffix, is not graphic at

5

all except in the fanciful sense of drawing with light—this is not to begrudge photography its due place in the pantheon of the fine arts. Typography is truly a graphic art only in respect of the drawing of the letter by the artist (calligraphy) and the cutting of it on the punch (engraving). The printmaking methods are of course graphic arts, but in varying degrees as they employ less and more draftsmanship by the artist on the stone, plate, woodblock, or whatever.

So much for definitions. Now, how do we find these arts placed in respect of education?

The graphic arts occupy two quite distinct hemispheres, often contained in the same university. One of them is given over to the history-of-art people and the graphic arts appear (however peripherally) in the academic courses primarily devoted to masters and styles of painting in western Europe from the Quattrocento to the new world and the present time. Under the direction of professors, curators and docents it presents orderly successions of lectures and slides, print study room and gallery exhibits, and readings in textbooks. Works of art are named, their qualities discussed, attributions are assigned, influences pointed out—and sometimes irrelevancies such as rarity and market value creep into the dialogue between teacher and student.

The other hemisphere is the realm of the artist, the maker (latterly known as the creator). It is studio-land, daubed with ink, littered with paper, cluttered with presses. Here deeds not words count. The ultimate in verbalization is the praise-word "exciting." Over in the administration the deans like to talk about "creativity" in this connection.

Then there is the underworld, which I mention only in passing since it touches the liberal arts college, in this morning's context, obliquely if at all. It is the vast rumbling complex of ad men, type directors, quickie platemakers; of electronic eyes peering through film, pressure-sensitive Prestype for cold composition, Bourges tints, rubber cement and dragon's blood. Its frenetic population nevertheless proclaims that here is the homeland of the graphic arts indeed.

My particular assignment, within the spheres of the graphic arts we have just loftily surveyed, is to consider their possible relationship to the liberal arts college undergraduate. This immediately brings us down to cases; the pointing hand in my instructions—in addition to forceful jabs in the direction of the clock—clearly indicates that I am expected to talk about my work at a certain small college. What have I been doing since 1937 when the art faculty at Dartmouth took me in?

The question surprised me once when I was so absorbed at my desk I didn't notice the approach of a pair of very important persons—one the exalted executive of a great foundation with fathomless power to do me good:

"What would you say is the underlying philosophy of your graphic arts program—the courses, the print collections, the workshop and all?"

"Well . . . ," I choked. "It's so that no student needs to die wondering about the graphic arts."

The great men moved on without another word, without doing me the least bit of good. I was much younger then, more impressionable and easily stage-frightened, no doubt. What would I say now if you asked me (and you have, through the demands of our host) what I've been about during the past thirty years? The answer would sound facetious—and would be equally unproductive of foundation bounty—if I replied, as I might very well do, that I've been devoting myself to the confusion of the arts. Nevertheless there is truth in it.

But here I do not mean the ignorant misapplication of good tools and materials, or methods, in studio practice. Except for

7

purposes of candid experimentation (and I agree with Gabor Peterdi *that* has about reached its useful limit), I deplore reckless violation of proper boundaries, as between one traditional medium and another. I reject, profanely and emphatically, the tendency towards homogenizing all sorts of prints under the heading *graphics*. Rather, the confusion I am advocating would relax the anesthetic *cordon sanitaire* that separates the study of prints as art history from at least some varied, elementary practice of printmaking. This is recommended not as self-expression or for any supposed recreational or therapeutic benefit, but expressly for the understanding obtained, by this and by no other means, of the master printmakers and their work.

For the student—as a means of penetrating the subject more thoroughly than is possible by the usual separate approaches and at the same time warming the learning process with personal feeling—the combination of historical, literary and critical, with practical, makes for economy of effort and the rewarding sense of accomplishment that drives him on. He can never really see what is in a pull from a Rembrandt plate until he has pulled one from a plate of his own; however unworthy of comparison, it opens his heart to form a common bond with the old Dutchman. And though, as compared with art schools, the liberal arts college is bookish and therefore more in need of practical leaven, the combined program deepens and enriches the committed young artist too.

After the question, what do I think I'm doing? comes the next question, how did I ever get into this anyhow? The diversion is welcome, though the answer is hardly simpler. In my fourth grade room a fat red 1912 specimen book of the American Type Founders stood on the window shelf next the unabridged Webster. I spent hours studying it; I was already fascinated by letter forms. My father once observed that I might turn out to be an engraver of letters. Years later when I asked him what put that into his head, he said, "Weren't you forever copying inscriptions and making little manuscript books?" "Yes, I suppose so. But did you ever know a letter-engraver?" "Oh yes, very well. A schoolmate of mine and a clever one." "So what became of him?" "Well, as a boy he got so smart at drawing five-dollar bills he could pass them off. Then, I think while he was in prison the first time, he learnt higher denominations and even practised engraving. He was one of the best in his line, but he's been most of the time in the pen."

I never took up that line. I did, however, get a job as printer's devil in a firm with the strait-laced name of Lane-Miles Standish, where one of my duties was to lug a five-gallon can of war-rationed type wash round the corner to fill up the tank of the boss's car. Neither of us went to jail for that. During the summer, after school, and on Saturdays I continued with an apprenticeship that progressed from delivering finished work and sweeping the floor to distributing pi, setting type, slip-sheeting runs on the cylinder press and feeding a jobber. When I went to the university, I landed a part-time proof-reading job at its press, working nights. There was in the corner an idle Washington hand press on which I produced a few illustrated Nash incunabula of simplest format. My young artist aunt gave me a start on cutting blocks, and her accomplished husband pointers on etching. Experiments with the other printmaking surfaces had to wait for a bit.

The Graphic Arts Workshop began when we were in New York and I bought an old Washington hand press of my own. That was thirty-five years ago. No one knows how many migrations it had survived before I trucked it over from the Brooklyn warehouse and then later from New York to Hanover to set it up in the basement room of Baker Library. There it served faithfully the generations of students until, in the recent move to Hopkins Center, Buildings-and-Grounds lost

9

control and allowed it to pitch to the concrete floor. When I bought that press in New York, we fortunately did not have to fit it into our Patchin Place apartment. Word of my plan had reached Alvin Johnson; and he led me to the roof of the New School for Social Research on West 12th Street and into the best lighted, roomiest penthouse studio imaginable. Would this do? We took over at once, and, giddy with good luck, laid out our resources in fonts of Caslon Old Face. My vision had been limited to a personal or rather family workshop, a place for experimenting and trying out projects at the design stage, for we were free-lancing. Dr. Johnson, however, put me in the catalogue for that autumn with courses. Being an instructor in art, but with only the sketchiest of formal training or apprenticeship—two or three undergraduate courses in design, and hanging around the Beaux Arts during our winter in Paris—I resolved to study. The graduate school in New York I thought would do turned me down. Meanwhile I continued teaching, and haunting print rooms and libraries, till the chance came to move press and baby and all up north. Harvard graduate school was warm and welcoming, first in the person of Paul J. Sachs, and then of Jakob Rosenberg. Under these professors I learned at least what insights a knowledge of the history of prints could yield. The great collection of the Department of Printing and Graphic Arts in the Houghton Library was an ever-growing resource, and the friendship of the man responsible for it, Philip Hofer, whom I had known in New York days, gave constant encouragement to my efforts.

The Graphic Arts Workshop at Dartmouth, now located on the lower level of the Hopkins Art Center, is equipped very much as it was when first established at the New School. One important addition is a Vandercook precision proof press. The Washington hand press (a replacement) is in constant use nevertheless and is, of course, essential to any full-sheet or large half-sheet bibliographical projects. It is most used for the big color woodcuts just now in vogue. A third press for the relief surface is a medium-size motor driven jobber which we are installing in the space long occupied by a highly experienced but loose-jointed treadle press. We expect to use this one for the illustrated books and booklets in smaller formats that are unsuitable for working on a proof press and that might tie up the hand press for long periods.

The types for these presses are laid in upward of a hundred cases. The most complete is the Caslon Old Face, based on the New School start, strengthened by direct imports after the workshop came to Hanover, so that a full range of roman and italic from eight- to forty-two-point is at hand. The roman fourteen-point (traditionally the "english" size) is supplied with long s and its ligatures for bibliographical fidelity in setting pre-nineteenth-century texts. For the same kind of work with old texts we aspire to an authentic black-letter, and thanks to the good offices of Harry Carter, archivist of the University Press, Oxford, and of James Blake, of the foundry at Sheffield which has the old matrices, we expect before long to have a couple of sizes of Antique Black, with all the auxiliary sorts, safely in our cases. That will be one typeface we shan't have to worry about mating to an italic!

Another typeface, in much smaller quantity, we have from that remote time in New York, is Futura Medium. We still think it is the best of the sanserifs and have never been tempted to lay in another. It was first employed in planning the cover of a new journal, the *Economic Forum*; if the typography was up to the merits of the editor, William McChesney Martin Jr., it was a resounding success. Finally, among the font materials we brought up from the city, was a set of Weiss initials, and various little treasures, e.g. a pair of star-like ornaments cut on engraver's blanks by my old friend, (Arthur) Allen Lewis.

11

The next typeface, in half a dozen sizes of roman and italic, to go in our cases was Centaur and Arrighi (the Monotype cutting; we acquired the distinguished Frederic Warde version thirty years later). This was ordered from Mackenzie & Harris to make a memorial broadside, commissioned by the Fogg Museum of Harvard for the Naumburg Room (where the Museum course used to meet), and was one of the early jobs completed in the workshop at Dartmouth. Then we imported a range of Perpetua roman, with emphasis on the larger sizes and titling letters. We came into a font of fourteen-point sloped Lydian Bold that Mark Lansburgh purchased to print a small book and generously donated when he was graduated. Other benefactions have come from the casting room of The Stinehour Press—a useful array of Monotype Bembo and Goudy Modern—and a particularly distinguished gift was the Benner Greek by its designer Francis Fobes, late professor of classics at Amherst and master of the Snail's Pace Press. As we turn from the relief surface, the curious visitor may like to know that those cartons piled high on the paper storage cabinet are packed tight with woodblocks cut or engraved—and abandoned—by students.

There are two intaglio presses. A doughty old star-wheel was found waiting in the catacombs of Carpenter Hall. For smaller plates there is a neat Weber Professional. The mortality of blankets, through carelessness on the part of novice printers, seems unnecessarily high and one young giant broke the teeth out of a gear-wheel of the smaller machine. Still, we don't agree that a merely technical studio attendant would be the satisfactory solution.

The planographic department, represented by a lithographic hand press of medium size, is handily located next to the sink, underneath which there is a cabinet loaded with stones, all ready—for graining.

In front of the windows is a long work-table at which up to ten men can sit before their work. In summer term only, may some of these chairs be occupied by girl students. My initial experience of this revolution at Dartmouth came last summer. Perhaps it was because such bright and attractive young women attended the lecture course I gave on sabbatical at Oxford last winter that the innovation was unexpectedly pleasing. I have always regarded coeducation tolerantly for daughters; now I am almost convinced a summer term of it may be good for sons too.

The tour of the Graphic Arts Workshop ends in a room off to one side containing desk, chair, and filing cabinets full of students' work and records, map cases and print boxes, and a disorderly heap of proofs from the latest projects and boxes full of odds and ends on their way somewhere, but where? This completes our first hemisphere, the practical, experimental, experiential side of a graphic arts program for the liberal arts undergraduate.

In order to look over the other hemisphere, the historical, literary, critical side of the same program, we cross the College green from the Hopkins Art Center to the Baker Library and go upstairs to a fair-sized seminar room and adjoining office, both lined with shelves full of books and print cases. For the most part the books are reference works divided into four categories: bibliography and books about books; typography and history of printing; prints and printmaking, design; history of the alphabet and calligraphy. There are many informal supplementary collections, e.g. of printing specimens from Plantin's press to those of Carl Purington Rollins's Dyke Mill; of fifty fine master prints under glass, the Wade Collection, from which selections are continually being arranged in the recreational reading rooms, with exhibition notes, by members of the graphic arts courses. Lying about for students to examine, are attractive and instructive pieces, such as blocks engraved by Thomas Bewick and Leonard Baskin; a kit of venerable wood-engraving tools presented by Rudolph Ruzicka; an engraving pad of Bruce Rogers's given by Joseph Low; a hand mould for casting type, brought here many years ago by Pierre Oly, together with an accumulation of punches, matrices, and cast letters at different stages of completion.

Enough has been said to indicate the strategy. Now this is how we proceed. The College offers, in the department of art, regular credit courses in graphic arts, advertised in the catalogue more or less as follows:

Book Design and Illustration. The development of books as art forms, and the sources of their design features, are studied in lectures, discussions, readings and practice. The course outlines major graphic and pictorial systems to the Renaissance, including classical inscriptions and medieval illuminated manuscripts. Fifteenth-century papermaking, woodcut, engraving, printing types and the calligraphic styles on which they were based, illustrated books and separate prints, are studied in detail.

In the graphic arts workshop students gain an understanding of techniques and materials by means of individual projects in block-cutting, plate-making and printing, and typography. Open to sophomores, juniors, and seniors.

Prints and Printing. From Dürer and the Renaissance masters of woodcut and engraving, this course surveys the development of the graphic arts to modern times. Rembrandt's etched work is studied in contrast to that of academic portrait engraving in the seventeenth century and the emerging modern spirit is traced in Goya's and Blake's genius expressed in prints. New processes are examined, including lithography as used by Daumier and Currier and Ives, and wood-engraving as practised by Bewick and the American school. The course closes with a critical review of contemporary printmaking and typography. w.

14

Graphic Arts Workshop.
Advanced study: A restricted program adjusted to individual needs
and interests of students of proved ability. Graphic arts of any period
and area may be the subject of concentrated study in seminar or
studio. May be re-elected for a second term.

In this way we have the means of holding on to a good man for
at least four terms. And if he comes along nicely, by that time
a hint may be dropped in his ear that a senior fellowship devoted to the big graphic arts project he has dreamed of could
be very worthwhile, the ideal opportunity and situation for
putting the two hemispheres solidly together. Then there is the
possibility of a summer internship at The Stinehour Press tug-
ging him in one direction and a winter on a Plantin-Moretus
Museum fellowship, in Antwerp, calling him from another.
And beyond that the life full of making and learning among
prints and books. (*pace* Dr. McLuhan.) How can the student
escape? Who would want to?

The Education
of a Graphic Artist

THE first graphic artist, whoever he was, had the revolution-
ary idea of producing a multiple! To get his message across to
a multitude of people he first thought of cutting into a block of
wood, of inking it, and impressing it onto a piece of paper. To
produce many thousands of prints from a wood block, such as
the image of Buddha, commissioned in 770 A.D. by the Empress
Shōtoku, was a worshipful act designed to accumulate merit
a thousandfold in the hereafter.

Perhaps we still should think of the merits, or demerits, we
might tot up in our own hereafters. The deluge caused by our
modern image makers, the advertising agencies, the tabloids,
the TV and film producers, might one day inundate us all—
making us into passive receiving sets unable to do our own
thinking and our own transmitting.

That little piece of wood, stone, or metal on which the graphic artist creates his image, his imprint, has a strong innate power,
for good or evil. It holds that power for the counterfeiter who
can produce and circulate his own currency, for the pornog-
rapher or for the demagogue, who can pollute people's minds.
It holds that strange fascination for any artist who can duplicate
his creation and send it out into the world, to carry his message
into the homes of people—and reach into their hearts and minds.

For better or for worse, this is what a print, or for that matter
any graphic reproduction can do, once it has left the artist's

16

studio or the publisher's printing press. If the artist turns publisher in the Old Testament sense of the word, he assumes a heavy responsibility. He can choose to publish truth or falsehood.

Scratch an artist born to graphics and you find a missionary, a zealot, a fanatic with a message—a budding Goya, Daumier, George Grosz—a man possessed by ideas and images, consumed by curiosity, haunted by a conscience.

Where does his education begin—where does it end? With this artist it began with the first image drawn on a lithographic stone, as an apprentice in a printing shop in the ancient city of Cologne.

Unforgettable sensation, the first print peeled off a piece of limestone—*my* own print, smelling of fresh delicious printing ink—ready to go out into the world.

The education of a young artist fifty years ago: grinding stones, one against the other, until they shone again as on the day they were quarried.

Grinding ink, for hours, until the black substance was dissolved in distilled water, smooth as velvet—ready to be used on the clean stone's surface.

Between kicks and curses, coming from the journeymen printers, between fetching breakfast for them and washing dishes, watching what makes a lithograph—and finally, after a long wait, being permitted to draw on the stone—your own design—a label for a wine bottle (Piesporter Tröpfchen) in three colors! The glory of it! And the excitement of secretly taking home small lithostones to indulge your own dreams: to become another Daumier! And how did Daumier do it? Haunt the streets and alleys, the courts and the smoke-filled rooms of Paris for firsthand encounters with the law, the wheeler-dealers, the bourgeois, and the workers.

So I haunted the narrow streets of old Cologne for similar

subject matter, frequented the zoo for comparative studies of man and beast, filled sketchbooks and went home to commit my findings to the stone.

No Daumier yet—but I was filled with enough curiosity and zeal to forge ahead, get the apprenticeship behind me, and enroll as a full-fledged art student in the great Academy of Graphic Arts in Leipzig, an institution unique in the world, entirely devoted to the art of the book, in a city considered the center of European publishing. What was then an art student's educational background would today be considered equivalent to a good college prep school education, fortified by an unusually active general interest in art, literature, and good music, classical and contemporary. All this fed and fired the imagination of the young graphic artist. The first—and what we thought the last—world war had demolished the old patterns, provoked new thinking, opened new vistas. In Leipzig the old met the new. We heard Bach's cantatas at St. Thomas Church, where the master himself had played the organ and conducted the choir—but we also attended the exciting premiere of Stravinsky's *Petrushka*. We heard Pinder lecturing on the Renaissance, but we also saw the first irreverent and invigorating exhibitions of Dada, our first collages, our first Mondrians and Picassos. Years of the great inflation, 1921–1923, years of starvation and exhilaration for the young madcap students, who read Dostoevsky and Kafka, Hölderlin and Strindberg, Hamsun and Upton Sinclair. We listened to the great Furtwängler in the Gwandhaus concerts, discussed Nietzsche, drank cheap wine, and danced to Paul Whiteman's jazz records till early in the morning. Some of us collapsed for sheer lack of sleep and nourishment, but that didn't squelch our lust for life.

All this, I always felt, belonged well to the education of the young graphic artist. It nourished our souls if not our bodies, it supplied us with ample material for the art of the book, made

18

us literate, and sensitive to the heartbeat of our time. The Academy furnished the tools, the technology. It became the laboratory for our first graphic efforts. There were workshops in etching, wood engraving, woodcut, and lithography, taught in the most orthodox way possible, thoroughly, traditionally, without any chance for experimentation. There were workshops in typesetting and book design, the only courses where the word "design" was used—and there were of course the usual supplementary studio courses in drawing and painting—no barnstorming here either. The quality of all these offerings was assured by the names of the Academy: the distinguished director, Walter Tiemann, type designer and bookman, Hugo Steiner-Prag and George Matthey, book designers and illustrators with an international reputation—and Professor Pinder, great authority on the Renaissance and star of our art history lectures. There also was Jan Tschichold, brash young classmate of mine, who laid the foundation for his new typography—based on Bauhaus functionalism, on Mondrian's geometric division, using stark and sober type deprived of all frills and serifs. Shades of Lissitsky's and Rodchenko's bold typographic experiments in Moscow, not far away in time and space! Deeply involved with the visual world of Holbein, Dürer, Goya, and Daumier—stirred deeply by my first encounters with the tortured characters of Kafka and Dostoevsky—I did my first lithographs for *Crime and Punishment*, tried my hankering for significant satire on *Gulliver's Travels*, and did my first wood engravings for *Tyll Ulenspiegel*, all of them—to my never-ending surprise—printed and published while I was still a student at the Academie.

Ten years of experimentation with life followed, years of love and marriage, trying my hand in journalism, playing "roving" artist-reporter, writer, and cartoonist, money pouring in—a lost weekend, culminating in a gigantic hang-over and disenchantment with my native land and its political she-nanigans—until history took a hand and forced a sudden exit, courtesy Alois Schicklgruber, amateur artist from Austria. First to Latin America, still as an artist-reporter, then to the North American continent—to an idyllic place called River-dale, close to the monstrous city of Manhattan—and a tough beginning under the shadow of a thing called Depression. A sobering shock that resulted in various salutary adventures—cartooning for *The Nation*—doing prints under the patronage of FDR's WPA—teaching graphics at Alvin Johnson's New School for Social Research and receiving my first American book commissions, by coincidence again *Gulliver's Travels* and *Crime and Punishment*, with side excursions into children's books, *Puss in Boots* and *Dick Whittington*, all done in my most be-loved medium, engraving on boxwood.

How does an artist get into the habit? Like a drinker to the bottle he feels himself drawn into the bliss of a medium that seems to be made for him. Tongue-tied before, all of a sudden he can express himself fluently, articulately. All inhibitions seem to be lifted and the spirit rises like new wine. To me wood engraving is an illumination. Light seems to emanate from the very soul of the piece of wood, released by the magic steel of the graver.

Perhaps second best, for me, is the lithographic stone—like wood an organic matter, mysteriously and patiently created by nature, in centuries of hoarding strength in its cells and mole-cules.

Art is a constant and continuous education, composed of minute day-by-day encounters and experiences—knowledge gained, knowledge stored, transformed—and passed on. Per-haps that is what ideally leads the artist to be an educator. His cup runneth over and he wants to share its abundance. (Not so ideally considered, teaching very often and obviously is part of an artist's sheer struggle for survival—but enough tired jokes have been made about this—i.e. "if you can't be an artist, teach!")

I remember how reluctantly I entered into my first compact with an educational institution. Stage fright, timidity to overcome, opinions to be formulated and authoritatively laid down! Heavens—what hypocrisy! All these private thoughts and doubts stored up in my mind, all of a sudden pulled out into the limelight, to be propounded like so many well-tested truths. Perhaps there is a slightly masochistic twist in many artists seriously engaged in teaching—forcing themselves to get out of the four secure walls of their studios to do battle, to be tested and see how well they stand up under questioning—to find perchance a few answers to some of their own doubts, and ultimately, hopefully, to come out on top.

I believe the worst species of teachers are those who face a class prepared and ready with all the answers to all those yet unasked questions. This spells contempt for the students and precludes an exchange of opinions. The teacher lectures in Olympian isolation—the students take notes, and questions are parried with ample quotes from famous books on the reading list. The best teachers are probably those individuals who never stop learning and have never stopped questioning themselves in the process of growing up.

But of course, ultimate success hinges on the teacher's unquestioned mastery of his own medium. My first baptism of fire occurred at the New School, before a small group of evening students, perhaps just as frightened and tired as I was after a hard day's work—housewives, commercial artists, school teachers in search of art with a capital A.

Let us skip charitably what is euphemistically called "adult education." The best one can do is to become friends with those tired, battle-scarred grown-ups and meet their problems individually and sympathetically on a group-therapy level.

Let me instead talk about my head-on collision with a real challenge—to teach graphic art to undergraduates in a professional art school. Twenty years ago, in New York's asphalt jungle, close to all the incredible art treasures of metropolitan New York. it was still possible to have such an art school without benefit of a graphic arts department.

I was lassoed into Pratt Institute by one of my finest friends, Khosrov Ajootian, then head of the Department of Illustration, who challenged me to start a graphics workshop from scratch.

I plunged into this venture with great innocence, but a lot of good will and youthful enthusiasm. Graphics and illustration were my business, my vocation, my life.

Memories of my student days at the Academy in Leipzig crowded my head, visions of workshops, where students pored over plates, stones, and blocks, the atmosphere charged with turpentine and nitric acid fumes; the clatter of printing presses, handmade paper stacked and dampened, waiting for the "bon à tirer"; and on the walls for inspiration prints of the great masters.

The scene opens in September, 1947, Brooklyn, U.S.A. The new graphics teacher tiptoes into the classroom to face his expectant students.

Where is the graphics workshop? There was none. "From scratch" was not a misnomer. No presses, no tools, no equipment, no precedent, no budget.

And so I started in a storage closet assigned to me as the only available space. Paintings, drawings everywhere but not a place to print. A few months later the first pieces of equipment were excavated from the basement of the Library School—an ancient derelict of a Franklin handpress, bedsize 14×18, and a case of Caslon Old Face, grimy and nicked. All this was solemnly installed in that little storage room.

My main effort: to get the students involved in typesetting, in block cutting, designing, and printing as quickly as possible. To start a publishing venture, by necessity on a minuscule scale, and send out proof to the world that a graphics workshop was operative at Pratt Institute.

I racked my brains for an appropriate name for such a hare-brained enterprise, which for lack of talented students, equipment, and financial support might be an abortion. I took no chances and called it the ADLIB Press, planning, with my fingers crossed, to publish each year at least one publication with my seniors, picking the best of the group and giving them as much freedom, under guidance, as I possibly could.

In 1951 we produced our first illustrated piece, a sixteen-page catalogue of a student exhibition, and one little gem of a book, *Kuz'ma*, a Russian folktale, handset and illustrated with color woodcuts by Dexter Knox, one of my most gifted students. He must have spent weeks by himself in that little workshop. In day and night shifts he produced six copies of that book, complete with slip case. Number one is my prized possession.

Everyone, including my friend Joe Blumenthal, the printer, in reviewing our space and equipment, or the lack of it, would throw up their hands and say: it can't be done!

The following year we started our first issue of ADLIB which came off the tiny handpress in the spring of 1953. Except for the cover, too large for our press, it was entirely produced by seven selected students, who worked as a team, chose their subject, designed and etched their own zinc relief plates, set type, and saw the issue through the press, in an edition of 200, I believe.

ADLIB was sent out to a carefully chosen group of leaders in the graphic arts and received a warm welcome.

It proved, plainly and simply, that these young artists were getting acquainted with some of the technical, artistic, and esthetic problems concerning the printed page, that all the complicated details of modern book production and page design could be better understood by actually handling the basic materials, type, plate, ink, paper, in a very simple set-up—and that there was a school in New York which provided that opportunity.

Little did people know *how* primitive our workshop was—but no matter: had I waited until the school could provide the ideal space and equipment, valuable years would have been lost and energy and enthusiasm dissipated.

I have seen schools with the most modern, up-to-date equipment, donated by the so-called Graphic Arts Industry in order to train artists for management or other commercial and not necessarily artistic purposes. I have rarely seen anything of importance being published by these technically overprivileged places.

I believe that to live up to certain limitations, to make do, to overcome technical difficulties and to improvise with makeshift and secondhand material, often generates creative thinking and creative doing.

With proof of our first efforts visible and well-received, with elbows out and eyes peeled for angels who might donate much-needed equipment, we slowly expanded our scope by boring from within. Traditionally art departments the world over always get the cast-offs and discards of the mother institution.

I can't recall that we had any piece of new equipment. We lived mainly on our ingenuity until I became chairman of the Department of Illustration, quickly renamed Department of Graphic Arts and Illustration, with its tail chopped off a short while later.

By that time it had become self-evident that "Illustration" had become a bad word due to commercial abuses in the magazine field. The department needed a broader esthetic basis, a face lifting, and the graphic arts could achieve just that.

The Department of Graphic Arts moved steadily upward,

24

with increasing confidence, with a steadily expanding faculty and mounting enrollment, with more space and equipment until my seven years program seemed completed and I felt free to move on to other ventures which I had started earlier.

A word about my students and my own approach to teaching (to avoid the word "method").

In the very beginning, finding them totally ignorant of the function and significance of the graphic media, I had to perform a one-man show—the "universal teacher." Tracing the development of literacy, the word made visible, man's urge to communicate and express himself in images, from Babylon to Picasso, I tried to present the panorama of a rich heritage that stretches across the ages. Looking through my early class notes I find that not only did I have to explain all the various graphic media but also their application to modern publishing and reproduction methods—from lithography to offset—from woodcut to line cut—from etching to photogravure—discussing problems of book design and book production—images wedded to type—mass production versus handpress—and so right back into our workshop.

The inspiration spadework done, I induced the students to find out something about themselves. My first assignment was an autobiographical statement, graphic and verbal—which yielded more often than not an astonishing variety of Americana.

The second assignment: to get out and see the world around them, the not-too-beautiful world of Brooklyn and adjacent boroughs—and come to terms with it mentally and visually. This induced the students to spend profitable days, individually, at the local fire station or police precinct, or to go out on a fishing boat at 5 A.M. and come back with the fishermen to unload at the Fulton Fish Market. Some spent a day in a Brooklyn brewery, or walked around the Williamsburg section, sketching and asking questions. Not all of them came back with masterpieces but some of them I saved for posterity in subsequent issues of ADLIB, which grew in popularity, was collected and embodied in libraries all over the world.

Other illustration problems were met in an assignment that called for a short children's book, which gave the student (if gifted) a chance to experiment with his own manuscript or with a given text or adaptation from the great treasury of children's literature. Here was an opportunity to experiment with bold design and color—not necessarily acceptable to traditional publishers, but perhaps a step in a fresh and original direction.

As the department grew, new courses were added to implement this ambitious program. Workshops in lithography, etching, and woodcut were added; lettering, calligraphy, and typography became necessary adjuncts. Space had to be found for presses, stone racks, type cases, and all the paraphernalia that goes with printmaking.

I maintain that the success of the department was largely due to the fact that it had become, in part, publisher of its students' accomplishments.

Needless to say, the students' education was entrusted to the hands of a large and distinguished faculty of painters, draughtsmen, sculptors, graphic artists, and designers, dedicated and sophisticated teachers, who laid the foundation for the senior projects. To which one must add a liberal arts program, culminating in a B.A. demanded largely by the parents and not necessarily making better artists of their children. What makes for better artists, it seems to me, in this our Twentieth Century, is an increasing awareness of the world around us, filled with sound and fury, violence and dizzying discoveries in science and technology.

The artist should be ideally a man of all seasons, alert and sensitive, inquisitive, compassionate. A large order.

What better chance is there for the young artist, within the framework of a university, to become acquainted with problems of engineering, architecture, biology, with the cross-currents in literature, in music, dance, and the theater which are so closely interwoven with the work of the graphic artist, the illustrator, the scenic designer?

The graphic art of our century seems so intricately related to problems of a structural, optical, scientific, or technological nature, that it is difficult to see how a young artist can cope with his world without a more than casual acquaintance with these phenomena.

Ideally all the arts should be under one roof. A university offers interesting possibilities through an exchange of ideas with engineers and zoologists, biologists and philosophers, poets and journalists.

What kind of work is open to the young graphic artist after graduation? Perhaps, instead of offering statistics and theories forced out of them, we might dig into our informal recollections of the recent past.

On the distaff side: let us eliminate those healthy cases who marry happily, bear children (perhaps artists)—or support a husband who is a struggling artist (also commendable)—or work (perhaps better childless) as part of a husband-wife team in the graphic vineyard. For either male or female the choice is wider than in any other field of art. Let's put the most uncompromising at the top of the list. Some of my most talented students become their own free agents, as painters, sculptors, printmakers, or combinations thereof.

An increasing number go into the publishing field, as illustrators of children's books, textbooks, magazines (the better ones)—as designers of paperbacks, book jackets, record covers, or less interesting matters. Some become skilled book designers or book-production people. Others, with a comic bent, turn cartoonist, or (less comic) take up careers as art directors. Those who work for advertising agencies are in the chips but usually lose their fine-arts touch.

Others turn up in art galleries, perhaps ultimately own them. Many, of course, go into teaching, usually on the high school, college, or professional art school level, thus closing a cycle, passing on their skills to the next generation. There are cases, not too desirable, where a young artist stays in the same school as student, graduate assistant, instructor, and retires ultimately as a greybearded professor.

In closing, a few words about the Pratt Center for Contemporary Printmaking which I started in 1956 on a small Rockefeller grant (and a prayer), at the instigation of Margaret Lowengrand, an artist and gallery owner. This too grew into an important focal point of graphic arts, Pratt's first extension into Manhattan, open to professional artists as an experimental graphic workshop.

I felt very strongly the lack of a studio-workshop, such as Hayter's Atelier 17 in Paris, in a metropolis like Manhattan which had become rapidly the art center of the world.

With printmaking offering strong competition to the other visual arts, where would the young art school graduate, the professional painter and sculptor be able to study and experiment in the old and new exciting graphic media?

With Pratt in a position of leadership what would be more logical than to sponsor a graphic center, open all day long, eleven months of the year, fully equipped to deal with every problem of printmaking in lithography, intaglio, relief, and all the fascinating new media offered by modern technology? What could be better as a by-product to attract international attention than having foreign artists and printers study and work at the center, exchange their experiences, and promote better understanding between nations?

Pratt Institute saw the wisdom of supporting this idea, with no academic strings attached to it, of a research laboratory for the mature artist in search of new contemporary graphic media. The idea caught on. The Center became a way station for artists from many countries of the world, working, studying, and taking back with them new and we hope favorable impressions of Pratt, of the U.S.A., and of its artists. The Center developed into an information agency for artists, collectors, foundations, and cultural organizations. It became a service center, printing editions for artists, museums, and galleries. It arranged exchange and travelling exhibitions, lectures and demonstrations on graphic arts, and perhaps most important it began to publish its own publication.

Again I began to think that without a publishing arm the Center would linger as just another workshop tucked away in a corner of vast Manhattan. How could we make our presence known and felt, how could we promote the idea of the contemporary print and its great potentials as a creative medium? How could we keep artists everywhere informed of new developments, new techniques, new concepts in today's printmaking?

I plunged into this venture with the same impatience and innocence of its difficulties as I had done previously at my Department of Graphic Arts. Publish I must and publish I did— on a shoestring and with the support of friends, Harold Hugo of Meriden Gravure Company foremost among them. Working on it without pay, in my free time, with the help of Bert Waggott and Andy Stasik, my young assistants, we launched the first issue in the spring of 1961, edition 2,500, as a semi-annual —and we have been going at it ever since. Now *Artist's Proof* has grown into a rather mature and elegant bound annual, edition 6,000, and with the professional know-how of Barre Publishers we hope to keep going for a long time.

Has it become clear to you that the print, the multiple, is here to stay and that I for one intend to stay with it?

Has it also become evident how mad an artist can be who wants to hang on to his own work, wants to continue to teach, to write—and to publish—all in one short lifetime? Perhaps proof positive that an artist can have his cake, can eat it—and have his fill without a stomach ache.

FREDERICK WALKEY

Graphic Arts Education:
A Museum Program

ON more than one occasion, I have been asked, "Is DeCordova a print museum?" The answer is no, but the question is not without foundation because prints have always been generously represented in our exhibition schedule. A review of the records reveals that from 1950 to the present we have had forty-eight print exhibitions. I was surprised to discover, because I hadn't remembered it myself, that the first special exhibition we had after the Museum opened in October, 1950, was a travelling exhibition from the Boston Printmakers' Annual Show.

In order to put my later remarks into context, it might be useful to present a brief historical review of the way the Museum came into being. When I arrived as its Director in 1949, the DeCordova was not a museum at all—it was merely a building. The remnants of Julian deCordova's collection remained, but they were in no sense the nucleus of a potentially significant collection nor did they offer guidelines for future collecting. Since the members of the Board of Directors did not have the conventional responsibility for the care and cultivation of a collection, they turned to Julian deCordova's will for guidance. "Education" was the key word they found, and education in art offered the Board two options: public exhibitions or art classes. They chose to do both, and for more than fifteen years the Museum has pursued these two directions.

Over the years the greater portion of our energies and funds have gone into developing the quality and significance of both the exhibition and class programs, and through these programs we have made a determined effort to give as many people as possible a significant involvement in art.

Before dealing specifically with the Museum's educational activities in the area of the graphic arts, I would like to discuss some general aspects of "Education in the Graphic Arts." It seems to me that education in the graphic arts presents greater problems than any other art form, because graphics are more cerebral, less affecting in a physical emotional sense and require a more extensive technical understanding on the part of the viewer to be appreciated. The acknowledged major media, painting and sculpture, have an immediacy and a presence usually absent in the graphic processes. The traditional graphic materials, ink and paper, lack the variety inherent in paint or the obvious physicality of the sculptor's materials. Traditional attitudes, especially in America, have reinforced the view that a print is in the same category as a watercolor or pastel, in that a print has seldom been the vehicle chosen by an American artist to express a major statement. And this view still prevails among large numbers of the public, for we know there is not much glamour generated by the opening of a print exhibition. It may be that even under ideal conditions prints will always have a limited audience. It has occurred to me that prints may appeal primarily to people who have a special combination of interests—either to the literary person with a strong interest in art or to the artist with a literary leaning—for prints usually graphically illustrate the idea they deal with, while a painting can much more convincingly *be* the idea itself.

The landscape painter suggests air and its properties, light and its properties, water and its properties, more convincingly and therefore more persuasively to a general audience than does the printmaker. The scale of the print, too, has limited its appeal, for traditionally prints have not been made to serve as wall decorations; they have relatively little carrying power and do very little to alter or enhance the architecture of the room in which they are hung. (Considerable imagination is required to achieve a dramatic print-show installation.)

Offsetting these factors which tend to limit the appeal of the graphic arts are other factors which create an audience for prints. These positive factors are "availability," "craftsmanship," "duplication," and again, "scale."

By "availability" I mean the sense in which high-quality prints have always been available to the knowledgeable collector. For the novice collector, nothing was harder to find only five or six years ago in Boston than a good selection of prints for sale. Dealers wouldn't handle them because the unit profit was too small on each sale and because there was little prestige attached to handling graphics. Only in the past five years has the demand for prints encouraged local dealers to carry them. However, for the initiate, the established collector of old master prints or contemporary prints—the person who knew his way around the New York and Boston galleries, who subscribed to auction catalogues and who associated with other collectors—for such people good prints have always been available at the right prices. The simple fact was and is that a print which is struck in an edition of 50, 100, or more is more likely to be available than a unique work of art, and usually at a reasonable price. "Availability" also made it possible for quite a few people of relatively modest means to collect in depth. It was possible only a few years ago to make superb collections of twentieth-century German graphics for less than the cost of a modest Van Gogh drawing.

"Craftsmanship" in art has been somewhat de-emphasized recently, but it continues nevertheless to have an inherent appeal for most of us and it is found more abundantly in the graphic arts than in any other art forms today. In many cases, today's printmakers have become not only master craftsmen but even virtuosos in the manipulation of paper surfaces.

Although I said earlier that in the past the relatively small scale of graphic work has limited its appeal, in the case of contemporary prints the reverse is true. Contemporary paintings have become so large that they tend to destroy their own potential market, whereas contemporary prints are scaled more appropriately for contemporary American homes.

One might suppose that the element of "duplication" in the printmaking process would be a handicap, but it is in fact an asset. As long as the editions are not excessively large, works of art that are produced in duplicate receive a wide distribution in public and private collections and create a bond of interest among collectors. Differences, rarities, and conditions within the same edition serve to enliven interest, as one quickly learns from talking to any print collector.

These four qualities—"availability," "scale," "craftsmanship," and "duplication"—have helped to develop an informed and appreciative audience for print exhibitions at the DeCordova Museum. As a museum director, I find exhibiting prints an especially rewarding part of the program. Now that the Museum has been in operation for nearly seventeen years, and we have developed a relatively sophisticated audience, it is not necessary to shock or irritate our audience in order to attract attention. Among our 2,500 family members and among our thousands of casual visitors, there are many who apparently find the same satisfactions in a good print exhibition that I do. The DeCordova's influence as an educator in graphic arts derives from its activities in several areas: its publications, collection, exhibitions, gallery talks, lectures, and classes. At DeCordova we begin the education of our audience with the mailing pieces that go into their homes—announcements designed to stimulate and entice simultaneously, to give a foretaste of the exhibition or event which is being announced. For the casual visitor to the galleries there is no regular program of education. I believe that art speaks for itself, provided the installation enables the visitor to make contact with the artist. During each exhibition, the Curator of Education or his assistant gives a series of talks to various groups invited for that purpose. During a four-week exhibition, as many as 500 adults or school children may attend such talks. Neighboring schools bring busloads of children to the Museum to see major exhibitions, and each art class at DeCordova is encouraged to visit each new exhibition and receive a brief gallery talk from the class instructor. If we have not published a catalogue for the exhibition (and we usually do not for our smaller exhibits) someone in the Education Department prepares a one- or two-page information sheet on the artist and the work on view which is distributed free to all visitors.

As I said earlier, the Museum has presented forty-eight print exhibitions since 1950. In recent years, the scope of the print exhibition program has broadened to include work from all over the world and from different periods of the past. We have, for example, presented definitive one-man exhibitions of prints by Honoré Daumier, Leonard Baskin, Jacques Callot, Odilon Redon, Stanley Hayter, Gabor Peterdi, and Maurits Escher. Our group exhibitions have included "Three Centuries of Japanese Prints," "Contemporary Polish Graphics," "European Prints of the 19th Century," and "American Prints from 1920 to 1935" (from the Boston Public Library). Although we have not placed major emphasis on building a permanent collection for the Museum, the DeCordova has acquired the nucleus of a good collection of contemporary American prints. This collection had its beginning as recently as 1961 when we presented an invitational exhibition of 150 prints by fifty major American printmakers. Rather than awarding cash prizes, we announced that the Museum would buy a thousand dollars worth of prints from the exhibition. These "purchase prizes" were announced at the opening of the exhibit in order to stimulate other purchases. The exhibition was a dramatic success in terms of attendance and viewer response, and 102 prints were sold in addition to twelve purchased by the Museum. We had, by our lead, encouraged other buyers, many of whom had never before purchased a work of art. Since that time, the Museum has set aside a modest sum each year for the purchase of prints, and has regularly purchased prints from its own exhibitions and from other print shows presented in the Boston area.

I have said that one of our major goals at DeCordova has been to involve as many people as possible in art. The most immediate and intimate form of involvement is participation in art, the process of making art oneself. The DeCordova conducts a year-round program of art classes with a weekly enrollment of about 500 adults and 200 children and with a part-time faculty of twenty-six instructors. The underlying philosophy of our adult classes is the same as that which presumably underlies the best professional art schools. This philosophy demands from students a total commitment to their art. We know from experience that, given the opportunity, adult students in Museum classes will make the same commitment as so-called professional artists. The only difference between our school and a professional school is that it is not our purpose to produce professional artists, people who expect to make a living through art; but we do expect to develop amateurs who are as committed to art as the professional.

Instruction in printmaking is given in the DeCordova Print Workshop. The Workshop meets only once a week, but that once-a-week class lasts six hours. At each session varying

36

lengths of time are spent on experimentation, technique, and criticism. Group discussion and analysis count heavily in these sessions and distinguish an adult workshop from an art school, since many of the adult students have achieved maturity and a relatively high degree of sophistication in matters of art. Experimentation is extremely important for adults because it prevents a rigidity of attitude which so often pervades adult art classes. In conventional classes where students rely on learning the craft dogmatically from a master, they tend to become followers and consequently do not learn to think creatively. It may be that among students in the Workshop the frustration level is higher in the beginning since the rewards of achievement may be longer in coming, but the purpose of the Workshop is to develop the self-reliant artist who can function independently, apart from the stimulating environment of the workshop.

If students learn by seeing the work of professional artists, and they unquestionably do, then the students at DeCordova automatically have the advantage of viewing a whole series of varied, top-quality exhibitions. This year, in addition to two group exhibitions—the "15th Annual National Print Competition of the Brooklyn Museum" and "One-Cent Life" which included prints by European and American artists oriented toward the abstract expressionist movement—there were four one-man shows by major American printmakers—Antonio Frasconi, Carol Summers, Dean Meeker, and Leonard Edmondson. At least three more graphic exhibitions will be presented in 1967—prints by Michael Mazur, a group show of sixty prints by Canadian artists, and finally, eighty Goya prints, "Los Caprichos." In these nine exhibitions students will have been exposed to virtually all the technical possibilities in printmaking.

Finally, I want to return to the Museum's stated goal of involving people in art. A few years ago, to measure the degree of involvement which existed in our membership, we sent out a questionnaire to find out what works of art were owned by our Associate members. We were also trying to learn if there were any hitherto unknown collectors especially of contemporary art. The results of the survey were gratifying. We found out that literally hundreds of our Associates owned works of art. True, most owned only a handful—a painting, a small sculpture, perhaps, and usually several prints. A file was made of these returns and from that file we were able subsequently to put together such print exhibitions as "German Expressionists," "Prints by Odilon Redon," "Henry Moore Graphics," and "School of Paris Prints." This widespread interest in prints within our membership suggested to us that it might be useful to form a DeCordova Print Club. Accordingly, a Print Club was organized to involve its members in several ways: 1) to present print exhibitions at the Museum of work owned by the members, 2) to present talks on prints by various experts, 3) to publish an irregular Print Club bulletin containing news of print exhibitions and information on prints, and 4) to organize field trips to museums or private collections to view and discuss prints under the guidance of Museum staff members. After the Print Club had been in existence for two and one half years, it became apparent that the demand for the above services was not confined to a small group of collectors. We found that a very large number of our Associate members were interested to some extent in most of the Print Club activities. Therefore we have ceased to sponsor the Print Club as a separate organization but are now offering all our Associate members the services formerly offered to Print Club members only.

We will continue to present occasional exhibitions selected from the prints owned by Associates; news of prints and print exhibitions will be published in our Associate Newsletter; lectures, films, and demonstrations will be presented in connection with print exhibitions and will be open to all Associates. Over the years we have learned a great deal about our members' interests and how to satisfy them effectively. We know that there is a growing public interest in prints and that there is within our membership a substantial involved audience for print exhibitions of quality.

INDEX

ing in the history of the graphic arts, 10

Hofer, Philip, 10

Images, mass-produced for present-day audience, 16; the image-producers, 6–7, 16

Johnson, Alvin, 10, 20

Knox, Dexter, his design, printing and illustration of *Kuz'ma*, 23

Liberal arts, defined, 5

Nash, Ray, boyhood studies of letter forms, 8–9; work as printer's devil, 9; first printing, woodcutting, etching, 9; beginning of Graphic Arts Workshop at New School for Social Research, 10; as typographer, 9–10; Graphic Arts Workshop at Dartmouth College, 10–13; lectures at Dartmouth, 13–15; a program allying study of prints as art history with the practice of printmaking, 7–8; influence of teaching, 3–4.

New School for Social Research, its courses in printing and the graphic arts in 1930's, 10

Photography, 5–6

Pratt Center for Contemporary Printmaking, 4, 28–29

Printing and the graphic arts, their place in American higher learning, 3; classroom teaching of printing and the graphic arts in American colleges, 6; studio teaching, 6; courses at Dartmouth College in Book Design and Illustration and in Prints and Printing, 14; teaching of printmaking, design and printing at Pratt Institute, Brooklyn, 23–26

Prints, as multiples, 16

Tschichold, Jan, 19

Typography, 6

Wade Collection of master prints, Dartmouth College, 13

Walkey, Frederick, his work as director of DeCordova Museum, 4. See also *DeCordova Museum.*

NAMES AND TITLES MENTIONED ONLY

One thousand copies have been printed for the
Boston Public Library by The Stinehour Press,
Lunenburg, Vermont, in June, 1969.